How It's Done

Building a House

by Wendy Hinote Lanier

FOCUS READERS

BEACON

www.focusreaders.com

Focus Readers is distributed by North Star Editions:
sales@northstareditions.com | 888-417-0195

Produced for Focus Readers by Red Line Editorial.

Content Consultant: Karen Chou, Ph.D., P.E., Assistant Chair and Clinical Professor of Civil & Environmental Engineering, Northwestern University

Photographs ©: Radovan1/Shutterstock Images, cover, 1; Andrew Ostry/Shutterstock Images, 4, 29; Steven Frame/Shutterstock Images, 7; bubutu/Shutterstock Images, 8; Dwight Smith/Shutterstock Images, 11; David Papazian/Shutterstock Images, 13; ungvar/Shutterstock Images, 14; Alhim/Shutterstock Images, 16; Red Line Editorial, 19; TexasPixelPro/iStockphoto, 20–21; TFoxFoto/Shutterstock Images, 22; Grigvovan/Shutterstock Images, 25; Andy Dean Photography/Shutterstock Images, 26

Library of Congress Cataloging-in-Publication Data
Names: Lanier, Wendy Hinote, author.
Title: Building a house / by Wendy Hinote Lanier.
Description: Lake Elmo, MN : Focus Readers, [2020] | Series: How it's done | Includes index. | Audience: Grades 4–6.
Identifiers: LCCN 2019025946 (print) | LCCN 2019025947 (ebook) | ISBN 9781644930366 (hardcover) | ISBN 9781644931158 (paperback) | ISBN 9781644932735 (pdf) | ISBN 9781644931943 (ebook)
Subjects: LCSH: House construction--Juvenile literature.
Classification: LCC TH4811.5 .L36 2020 (print) | LCC TH4811.5 (ebook) | DDC 690/.837--dc23
LC record available at https://lccn.loc.gov/2019025946
LC ebook record available at https://lccn.loc.gov/2019025947

Printed in the United States of America
Mankato, MN
012020

About the Author

Wendy Hinote Lanier is a former elementary teacher and a Texan through and through. She writes and speaks for children and adults on a variety of topics. She is the author of more than 40 books for children and young adults on topics related to science, technology, social studies, the arts, and, of course, Texas.

Table of Contents

Chapter 1

Before There's a House

It is early morning. The sound of heavy machines breaks the silence. A backhoe and a bulldozer chug to life. The big machines begin moving. They go back and forth across an empty lot.

A bulldozer pushes soil out of the way to clear space for a new house.

The bulldozer crawls along on its tracks. It clears away rocks, trees, and bushes. It pushes the soil to make the ground level.

The backhoe digs up tree roots. It digs a hole for a **foundation**. The backhoe also loads extra soil into a truck. The soil will be carried away.

Fun Fact

Bulldozers are huge machines. They are strong enough to pull fully loaded army tanks.

Backhoes dig up trees to clear a lot for a new house.

When the day is over, the lot is ready. A new home will be built there.

Chapter 2

From the Ground Up

At the lot, workers build a foundation. They make a wooden frame. Then they lay a **grid** of steel bars inside the frame. They pour wet concrete over the bars. The concrete hardens inside the frame.

Steel bars give a foundation extra strength.

The next step is to build the house's shell. The shell includes the walls and roof. Workers begin by building walls. Walls are made of **lumber**. Workers nail the lumber together on the ground. Then they raise the walls into place.

Workers build the roof next. They often use pre-built pieces.

Fun Fact

Some houses are built over a basement or crawl space.

Workers lift a new wall into place.

The pieces are made up of triangles. They give the roof its shape. This shape allows rain to roll off the house. A big crane lifts the pieces into place. Workers attach the pieces to the walls.

The house's shell is now ready. Workers cover the outside with sheets of plywood. The plywood gives the house a solid outer surface. It also helps hold up the roof.

Lastly, workers add windows and outside doors. They cover the

Fun Fact

When building houses, crews must follow codes. These rules for building help make houses safe.

A worker moves a pre-built roof piece into place.

shell with a waterproof material. The outside of the house is almost complete. Much of the remaining work takes place inside.

Chapter 3

Inside the Walls

When the shell is complete, the **plumbers** arrive. They put water pipes in the walls and ceiling. Drains go in the floor. Drains take away wastewater. Plumbers also put in bathtubs and showers.

Water pipes carry water throughout the house.

Tubes in the attic carry fresh air throughout the house.

Next, workers add the heating, **ventilation**, and air-conditioning (HVAC) system. Tubes carry warm or cool air throughout the house. Workers also put **vents** through the roof. The vents allow harmful gases to escape.

Then it's the electrician's turn. Outlets go in the walls. They supply power to lights and electrical items. Wiring connects the outlets to a breaker box. The breaker box controls the house's electricity. The electrician also adds wiring for cable TV, telephones, and other systems.

Next, workers add insulation to the walls. This material keeps the house cool in the summer. It also keeps the house warm in the winter.

Then workers add **drywall**. The drywall covers the plumbing, electrical, and HVAC work. Workers apply a coating to the drywall. The coating makes the walls smooth for painting.

Meanwhile, outside work continues. Workers add shingles or tiles to the roof. These materials

Fun Fact

The early plumbing, electrical, and HVAC work is known as roughing in.

CROSS SECTION OF A WALL

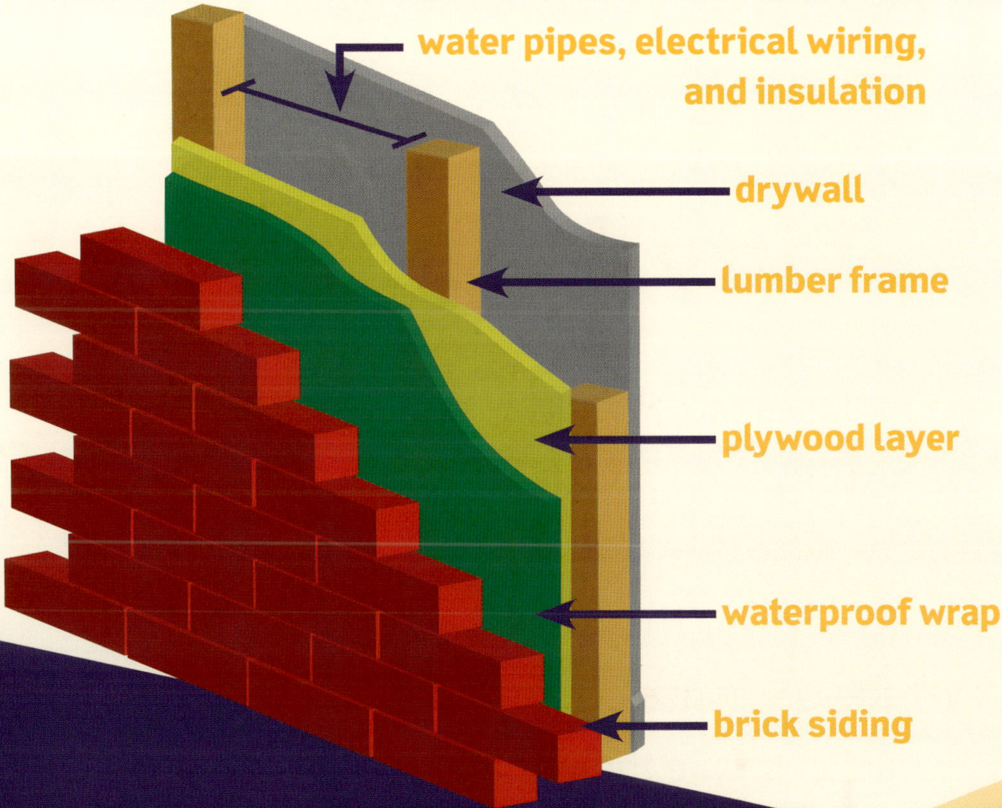

keep the inside of the house dry. Siding goes on the outside walls. This covering gives the house its own individual look. It is usually made of brick, vinyl, stone, or wood.

THAT'S AMAZING!

Tiny Houses

Tiny houses are amazing creations. They are popular with people who move often. Most tiny houses are less than 400 square feet (37 sq m). They are one-sixth the size of average US houses. Many are built on wheels. Owners can take their homes with them wherever they go.

Tiny houses take careful planning. People often use computer programs to make the plan. The programs let them see how the rooms fit together. People plan how best to use the space.

Some people build their own tiny house.

Chapter 4

Finishing Touches

When the walls are complete, the finish work can begin. Workers put cabinets in the kitchen and bathrooms. They add frames around the doors and windows. They hang all of the inside doors.

A worker adds a frame to the outside of a window.

Next, painters apply paint to the walls, cabinets, and frames. When it dries, workers put countertops in the kitchen and bathrooms. They add tile, carpet, or other flooring to all of the rooms.

Now the plumber, electrician, and HVAC workers can finish their work.

Fun Fact

Some homes are constructed using pre-built pieces. They can be built in days instead of months.

An electrician attaches wires and connects a light switch to the house's electricity.

The plumber puts in sinks, toilets, and faucets. The electrician puts in lights. Workers add **thermostats** for controlling the home's temperature.

Once approved, a finished home is ready for its new owners to move in.

At this point, the house is almost finished. Final details include mirrors, cabinet handles, and shower doors. Then a cleaning crew makes sure everything inside is spotless. Meanwhile, landscape workers add plants outside.

Building officials must approve the finished house. Sometimes there are a few final jobs. They might be things that were overlooked. Or they might be jobs that were not completed correctly. Workers complete these last-minute jobs. Then the house is finally ready for its new owner.

Fun Fact

A list of last-minute jobs or problems to fix is called a punch list.

FOCUS ON

Building a House

Write your answers on a separate piece of paper.

1. Write a paragraph explaining everything that is inside the walls of a house.
2. What do you think is the most important step in building a house? Why?
3. Why are thermostats put into a house?
   A. to adjust the music system
   B. to control temperature
   C. to open the garage door
4. What might happen if a house were made without insulation?
   A. The house might get very cold in the winter.
   B. The house might stay cool in the summer.
   C. The house might get too warm in the winter.

5. What does **apply** mean in this book?

*Workers **apply** a coating to the drywall. The coating makes the walls smooth for painting.*

- **A.** to try to get a job
- **B.** to put or spread on
- **C.** to work very hard

6. What does **level** mean in this book?

*The bulldozer crawls along on its tracks. It clears away rocks, trees, and bushes. It pushes the soil to make the ground **level**.*

- **A.** calm or unexcited
- **B.** bumpy or hilly
- **C.** flat or smooth

Answer key on page 32.

Glossary

drywall
A building material that is used for the inside walls and ceiling of a structure.

foundation
The supporting base of a structure.

grid
A series of crossed bars that create a surface of rectangles or squares.

lumber
Trees that have been sawed into rough planks for use in building.

plumbers
People who install and repair water pipes, drains, toilets, tubs, and faucets.

thermostats
Devices that control temperature.

ventilation
The process of allowing fresh air to enter and move through a room or building.

vents
Openings that allow air, smoke, or fumes to escape.

To Learn More

BOOKS

Alkire, Jessie. *Construct It! Architecture You Can Build, Break, and Build Again.* Minneapolis: Abdo Publishing, 2018.

Finger, Brad. *13 Skyscrapers Children Should Know.* New York: Prestel Publishing, 2016.

Howell, Izzi. *Buildings.* North Mankato, MN: Capstone Press, 2019.

NOTE TO EDUCATORS

Visit **www.focusreaders.com** to find lesson plans, activities, links, and other resources related to this title.

Index

Answer Key: 1. Answers will vary; **2.** Answers will vary; **3.** B; **4.** A; **5.** B; **6.** C